Old ANSTRUTHER

Eric Eunson

First Published in the United Kingdom, 1997
reprinted 2003, 2008, 2010
By Stenlake Publishing Ltd, 54-58 Mill Square,
Catrine, Ayrshire KA5 6RD
01290 551122
www.stenlake.co.uk

ISBN 9781840330007

Lifeboat Saturday collectors on Shore Street *c.*1910. The white building behind the lamp post is dated 1721, and now forms part of the Fisheries' Museum.

Introduction

The story of the parishes of Anstruthers Easter and Wester, Kilrenny, and the villages they contain, has been the subject of some of the best local histories published in Fife in recent years. Several of these are listed in the bibliography, and I make no pretence of presenting only a basic sketch of this immensely historic area. This book is primarily a collection of images of Anster past, and despite the changes the past 100 years have wrought most will be reassuringly familiar to those who know and love this 'lang toun'.

The first mention of the fishing grounds off the May occurs in 1150 when fleets of Scottish, English, Belgian and Gallic boats were regular visitors to the Forth. In 1170 the Norman Countess Ada, daughter-in-law of King David I, granted the church of 'Kilrethni' to the canons of Dryburgh Abbey, and the same foundation received a grant of the church of Anstruther (West) from William de Candela around the same period. In 1225 the canons resolved a teinds dispute with the fishermen of Anstruther, with the intervention of Pope Honorarius. This event not only establishes the existence of a community of fishermen at this date, but also suggests that the potential revenues from the enterprise were substantial for the time.

Permission to build harbours was given to Anstruther Easter in 1541 and Cellardyke in 1543; by 1600 fleets of small, half decked crears were travelling to the fishing grounds of the Western and Northern Isles from both ports. Both East and West Anstruther were given Royal Burgh status by James VI, in 1583 and 1587 respectively. Anstruther's most famous minister James Melville was also installed in the latter year. His manse of 1590 still looks over the town, and his hospitality to Captain Juan Gomez de Medina and his stricken Armada ship is one of the town's most famous stories. The diminutive village of Kilrenny was a Burgh of Regality before 1672, and elevated to a Royal Burgh in 1707.

The area's prosperity continued until 1651, when Oliver Cromwell routed the garrison at Dunbar and crossed the Firth into Fife. From 1651-1656 Anstruther was forced to endure the abuses of a roundhead garrison in the town. Homes and businesses were looted by the English, and even St Nicholas' Church was robbed and its bible cast into the sea. In 1654 plague ravaged the town, and seventy victims were driven out to the Billowness to die, their bodies hastily buried without even a winding sheet. The following year the harbours of Anstruther and Cellardyke were devastated by storms, and the remainder of the century was blighted by frequent and prolonged dearths of fish in the Forth.

Although in 1670 only three ships belonged to West Anster and none to her neighbour, the fishing fleet had recovered to a strength of twenty-four vessels by 1710. In the same year a customs house was established, but the sheltered creek at the mouth of the Dreel remained a favourite spot for smugglers. During the first half of the eighteenth century the fleet of Cellardyke boats increased to fifty, but the industry was described as miserably decayed in 1790. Over the same period, the number of breweries in the town had fallen from twenty-four to just two or three.

Salt-cured herring was being produced in Anstruther in the early fourteenth century, on lands at the Harbourhead owned by the monks of Balmerino. It was this product which brought the fishing industry of Scotland exploding into prominence towards the middle of the nineteenth century. The Forth herring fishings fell into two seasons. The Lammas Drave lasted from August to September and rose to its peak between 1836-62, although it had virtually ceased by 1914. The winter herring were pursued during the first three months of the year, and as the summer fishing declined they grew steadily in importance. From the mid-nineteenth century, until the peak year of 1936, Anstruther became established as the herring capital of south-east Scotland. In 1840 the port boasted a fleet of 100 fishing boats, each with a crew of five men. At that time herring and pickled cod were being exported to London and Liverpool. Whaling from Anstruther began in the 1840s, but was important for only a few years, being abandoned in the 1860s. From 1845 the Anstruther and Leith Steam Packet Company ran paddle steamers serving the coasting trade between the East Neuk ports and Edinburgh. Salted herring from Anstruther was among the staple cargoes of their vessels (the *Stirling Castle*, *Xantho* and later the *Forth*). In 1859 the combined fleets of Anstruther and Cellardyke numbered 150, rising to 173 a year later. The fishing brought with it the establishment of a host of ancillary businesses including cooperages, curing establishments, cork works, chandlers and oilskin makers.

Construction of a new east pier at Anstruther began in 1866 and work continued for the next three years. Between February and March 1870, some ninety feet of it was destroyed by storms, with further damage occurring in October. In use by 1871, the pier was breached twice more before finally being finished in concrete in 1873. The West Pier, completed in June 1876, was made entirely of concrete earning it the nickname the 'potty pier'. During the 1890s steam fishing boats were introduced to Anster and by 1913 sixty steam drifters, mainly owned by Cellardyke skippers, belonged to the port.

Although restricted by the First World War, the herring industry continued to grow until 1936, a year of record catches. In 1929 the three independant burghs were unified into one under a single town council. The inner harbour was deepened and the west pier widened twice, but the winter herring shoals mysteriously deserted the Forth after the war, as periodically they had done before. The herring fishery effectively ended in 1947, although isolated catches continued to be landed for a few years thereafter. Anstruther's importance as a working harbour rapidly declined.

Since the 1950s Anstruther's history has shared much with the other former fishing communities of the east coast. Tourists first discovered the area in significant numbers a hundred years earlier, when the steamers of MacGregor and Galloway began opening up the Fife coast to Edinburgh excursionists. Sadly this service ceased abruptly with the outbreak of the Great War and was not resumed. Today summer visitors account for much of the town's trade, but only provide limited employment, although a refreshing number of traditional family businesses still flourish. Some have suggested that the harbour should be converted into a marina for pleasure craft as has been done with great success at North Berwick, but to date this has never passed the speculative stage.

Eric Eunson, April 1997.

St Monans photographer William Easton took this picture of an open air service at Billowness around 1910. The prominent rock in the background is known as 'Johnnie Doo's Pulpit', and it is said that a youthful Thomas Chalmers came here to practice his skill as an orator. Stone from this area of foreshore was quarried in 1867 and used as infill during the construction of the east pier.

THE BATHING POOL, ANSTRUTHER

A.776

From the 1920s onwards the East Neuk villages came alive to the spirit of civic improvement, including the provision of amenities to cater for an ever increasing numbers of tourists. The Billowness Improvements Committee was formed in Anstruther in 1922, and five years later a bazaar was held in the Town Hall to finance the building of a bathing pool. This raised just £10 short of the £400 estimated cost. In 1933 children's play equipment consisting of three swings, a chute and an 'ocean wave' was installed ('ocean wave' seems to be an alternative name for the spinning conical death-trap I knew as a 'witches' hat'). The picture dates from 1934, a year before a second bazaar raised enough to double the pool in size. Sadly, high pollution levels have led to the abandonment of all Fife's seawater pools in the last twenty years.

BANKWELL ROAD, ANSTRUTHER.

98569.JV.

In 1919 Anstruther was one of the first towns in Fife to have plans for council housing prepared, and the homes in Glenogil Gardens were completed in 1921. The council's building programme was scheduled to coincide with a slum clearance programme centred on Shore Lane, Cards Wynd, Hadfoot Wynd and East Green, proposed in 1922 and eventually carried out four years later. In 1922 houses were completed in Fowler Place and Burnside Gardens, Cellardyke, with the unusual provision of pulleys on the gables to hoist fishing gear into the lofts, as in the traditional fishermen's homes. The third development of ten houses in Bankwell Road went ahead in 1924.

Although this postcard of Anstruther Wester from the north-west was sent in 1909, the Valentine of Dundee serial number in the corner dates the photo to 1889. Most of these buildings retain their seventeenth and eighteenth century frontages, but the rear elevations have almost all been completely rebuilt in twentieth century styles and materials. The Old Corn Mill in East Anstruther, left, dates from 1702 and is now a private house.

This 1908 photographer would be taking his life in his hands, standing in the middle of the road at the Buckie House corner today! Built in 1692, the exterior of Buckie House was covered with intricate patterns of shells during the nineteenth century by its owner Alexander Batchelor, a local slater. Robert Louis Stevenson describes how for a fee of thruppence, Batchelor would show visitors his extensive collection of shells, and the coffin intended for his own use, also covered in an elaborate shell design. It is believed he was indeed buried in it when he died in 1866. A map of 1790 shows the area in front of the house as a market place with a mercat cross, but this was probably removed when the coast road was upgraded to a turnpike between 1790 and 1799.

PARISH CHURCH, ANSTRUTHER WESTER

Ninety years have seen few changes to the Esplanade. The former Anster Wester Parish Church was until recently used as a hall by St Adrian's, but has been found to be in need of urgent and costly repairs. The tower is mainly sixteenth century, but some parts may be 300 years older. In 1846 the rest of the building was extensively reconstructed. The mouth of the Dreel was known as Westhaven, and there was once a substantial harbour here. In 1670 disaster struck when it was utterly destroyed by a tempest. The storm also did considerable damage to nearby properties in Fore Street, which stood in front of the present sea wall and contained some of the town's finest houses. Comprising nearly a third of the burgh, Fore Street had been completely washed away before 1700.

Although the Leven and East of Fife Railway was completed from Thornton to Leven in 1854, and extended to Kilconquhar in 1857, it was not until 1 September 1863 that the line finally reached Anstruther. The L&EFR was taken over by the North British Railway in 1877, and it was they who finally linked the town to St Andrews in 1883. This view looking west along the platforms was taken shortly after the NBR became part of the London & North Eastern Railway in 1923. Following the introduction and rapid expansion of bus services to and from Anstruther in the 1920s, the remoteness of the station from most of the population led to a decline in passengers. The railway still remained busy with freight as it was essential to the movement of fresh fish to the cities and inland towns.

When local man Andrew Waid died in London in 1804, he left the bulk of his money and property to twelve trustees for the purpose of erecting an academy in his home town 'to educate, clothe and maintain poor orphan boys and seamen's sons'. It was to remain unbuilt for over eighty years, but was eventually completed to a design by David Henry of St Andrews in 1886. The tower was originally intended to have a spire, but this extravagance was never carried through. 'The Waid' was taken over by Fife Education Authority and extended to the rear in 1930-31.

East Anstruther looking north-west from the Waid Tower in 1904. The pantiled farm buildings on the left have made way for the Farm Court housing development. In the centre are the tower of St Adrian's Church (1634) and the backs of the houses in Melville Terrace. On the far right is the former primary school, designed in 1900 by Williamson & Inglis of Kirkcaldy. It became an annexe of Waid Academy in 1924, and Fife County Council provided it with a drab extension in 1955.

Anstruther. Chalmers' Birthplace

Although this cottage is chiefly noted for being the birthplace of Thomas Chalmers in 1780, his family vacated it before 1786. Between 1848 and 1851 it housed the post office and the access pend to the High Street is still known as Old Post Office Close. By 1884 the house was 'dingy and dilapidated', but was saved from ruin and restored by Robert Fortune, a chemist and lay preacher. It had again fallen into disrepair by the mid 1960s, and continued to deteriorate. In 1979 it was bought by the National Trust, and later sold to W. Murray Jack who restored it in the early 1980s.

Elizabeth Gourlay was styled 'Anster's Oldest Newsagent' in this picture postcard of 1910, which she very possibly sold. The business was situated in the old property, dating from 1631, at the corner of Rodger Street and High Street. Elizabeth took it over from her late husband George some time between 1889 and 1893, and continued as proprietrix until around 1911. Pointedly, the headlines on the newspapers speak of 'Servian (Serbian) Atrocities', a reminder that Balkan conflicts are not a recent development.

The house on the far left was converted into a shop in the 1960s, but apart from the absence of congestion Rodger Street has hardly changed since this picture was taken around 1900. The street was part of the route of the Anstruther to St Andrews turnpike road, authorised in 1807 and completed four years later. During the 1840s passengers could travel the route thrice weekly in a curricle, a light two wheeled carriage drawn by two horses abreast.

Rodger Street looking north in 1906. The corner building on the far left, presently occupied by the TSB, is dated 1870. A couple of doors up the premises of George Doig, chemist (established 1854) sport just one of the town's immaculately preserved late nineteenth century shop frontages. The High Street and Rodger Street area possibly contain the best selection of these to have survived in the whole county, boasting many fine examples of woodworking, cast iron, engraved glass and terrazzo mosaic entrances.

At the Sands, Anstruther

The former Georgian coach house at the corner of Castle Street was converted to a modern home in the 1960s, but otherwise nothing much has altered significantly since this view was taken around 1908. The cart probably belongs to a farmer gathering seaweed for fertiliser. I am sure every resident of the area would love to see this environmentally friendly practice resumed, in the hope that it might cure the sulphurous stink that presently blights the Dreel in summer!

THE CROSS, ANSTRUTHER

78390. (JV)

The Williamson Memorial drinking fountain photographed in 1914. Stephen Williamson was born on 23 June 1827 in a house, long since demolished, at 27 James Street Cellardyke. He was founder of the Balfour Williamson Shipping Line, and from 1880 to 1885 was the Liberal MP for the St Andrews Burghs seat (which included the East Neuk). He was instrumental in the building of Cellardyke Town Hall, the Chalmers' Memorial Church and Waid Tower, and responsible for clearing the debts of the harbour improvements at Anstruther. He died in 1903 at Copley, Cheshire. Sadly, the monument to this illustrious citizen was removed some years ago.

Shore Street, West Anstruther

The Queen Victoria Jubilee fountain was removed two years before this postcard was sent in 1927. Originally topped with a gas lamp standard, the town council ordered its removal as it had become 'insanitary - even for horses'. The two storey building on the far right was extensively modernised by the Leven Reform Co-operative Society who opened their new store here on 4 April 1936. The nearby three storey building with dormers on the roof was formerly the Victoria Hotel, and was home to the Anstruther Post Office from 1901 to 1989.

'Long live the King!' - Provost Oliphant proclaims the accession of King George V at the Mercat Cross on 10 May 1910. At his side are members of the volunteer militia, 'E' Company 6th (Fifeshire) Volunteer Battalion, Black Watch. In the background are the Williamson Memorial Fountain and the old shore dues office, demolished in 1936.

The serial number of this photo dates it to 1880, a fact confirmed by the date stone of the building on the extreme right, which was just nearing completion. The low white building three doors up was rebuilt in 1883. The yawl on left, *21 KY*, is clinker built, a method of construction in which the strength of the hull comes from the overlapping timbers rather than the frame. Yawls of this type subsequently all but disappeared from the harbours of Fife, in favour of carvel built boats where the hull strength came from the rigid internal frame onto which the planks were laid flush.

20

Shore Street. Anstruther.

The same view in 1932, with the yawl *Maggie (KY 106)* in the foreground and the Fifie *Restless Waters (ML 55)* moored at the quayside. The inner harbour was deepened in 1933 and 1937 and the harbour wall in front of Shore Street widened to its present breadth in the latter year.

A forest of masts belonging to Anster's fleet of sailing drifters around the turn of the century, the end of the heyday of the big sail boats. Although the nickname 'the folly' is now applied to the whole of the wall in front of Shore Street, it was first coined for the triangular area beside the Jubilee Fountain, which was built on a sandy area of foreshore which absorbed the impact of the incoming tide.

THE CROSS. ANSTRUTHER.

A similar view photographed about fifty years later, featuring a contemporary Alexander's bus. Throughout the 1920s and '30s this Falkirk-based bus group took over dozens of independent bus operators in Fife, soon creating a monopoly. Among the companies swallowed up was Thomas Gardner of Anstruther, who ran a fleet of buses from his Harbourhead Garage, now part of the Scottish Fisheries Museum, from 1922 to 1932. Behind the bus are the covered sale ring, harbour offices, public waiting room and lavatories, opened in 1936. They were demolished and a much needed replacement built in conjunction with landscaping improvements of 'the folly' in 1991.

The Chalmers' Memorial Lighthouse has guided vessels into Anster harbour since 1880. It was the gift of Mrs Hannah Harvey, who also financed the building of a rail on the harbour wall and a new lifeboat for the town. The yawls in this 1925 picture are, from left, the *Refuge*, *Enterprise*, and *Fisher Lassie*.

This study of a regrettably anonymous Fifie was taken at the East Pier by Charles F.S. Burrows around 1912. Burrows began taking studio photographs in a wooden shed at the rear of his newsagent's shop at 30 Shore Street between 1903 and 1907. A few years later he produced a number of Anstruther views as picture postcards, and these were followed by a series depicting the coast towns from St Monans to Kingsbarns in the 1920s.

FISHING, AT ANSTRUTHER.

Another Charles Burrows photograph at the East Pier c.1912, probably taken during the winter herring fishing. A Stornoway registered steam drifter, and the *Jeannie Brown,* a Dunbar Fifie have recently docked, and a crowd of fish buyers and spectators have begun to gather. A couple of lads cling to the beacon, no doubt announcing the names of approaching boats as soon as they come into view.

Probably only a few minutes have passed since the facing picture was taken, but the foreground is crowded with new arrivals and the clear sky beginning to cloud with smoke from the steam drifters.

By 1855 Anstruther was one of the most important curing ports in Scotland, a position it was to hold until the Second World War. Many of the women of the port followed the fleet during its seasonal voyages from Shetland to Lowestoft, for the essential task of gutting the herring on the quayside was invariably their job. The fish were poured into long wooden troughs called 'farlans', and the women worked in teams of three, two gutting and another packing the fish into barrels with alternating layers of coarse salt. An experienced gutter could clean sixty fish in a minute, with strips of rags bound around the fingers the only protection from the razor edged knives. This scene shows some of fish merchant John Bonthron's gutting crews on the Middle Pier c.1910.

During the summer of 1937 the contractor Robert Terras of East Wemyss began work on the deepening of the harbour's inner basin and the widening of the West Pier. A temporary concrete coffer dam, shown above, was built across the 'cut mouth' of the Middle Pier to prevent tidal flooding of the works. On August 25th, the West pier began to give under the pressure of water between it and the empty dock, causing a fissure 200ft long to open up. Repairs were carried out, but deepening work did not resume until the end of September. The coffer dam was blown up on completion of the scheme in December.

A Pittenweem Fifie moored at the East Pier attracts attention in this postcard, published by C.S. Russell of 56 High Street c.1910. In 1914 Charles Stiven Russell founded the *Coast Burghs Observer* (later *East Fife Observer*) which remained the main newspaper in the East Neuk until the 1950s. Part of Miller's boatyard, with a Fifie under construction on the slip, can be seen in the background. Miller of St Monans took over the yard from Jarvis in 1899, and it was sold to Alexander Aitken around 1920. Following his death in 1951 it passed to his heirs who eventually changed the name to Smith and Hutton. The business closed in the 1970s and the old premises have recently been converted into part of the Scottish Fisheries Museum.

It was the MP Stephen Williamson who encouraged Anstruther's fishermen to use steam vessels; the town's first, the *Maggie Lauder*, was launched in 1891. By 1904 eleven steam liners/drifters were owned by the port, a figure which had risen to thirty-five by 1928. Most of the steam drifters pursued the herring shoals in autumn and winter, switching to line fishing for white fish during the early summer months. In 1940 all the town's steam and motor boats were requisitioned by the Admiralty for war service. The photograph shows one of Anster's best known drifters, the *Spes Melior KY19*, in 1937.

This unique private snapshot was taken in July 1904, and depicts the last sailing of the lifeboat *Royal Stewart*. She was the gift of Hannah Harvey in 1888, and was replaced by the *James and Mary Walker*, a thirty-eight foot vessel powered by twelve oars which remained in service until 1933.

Lifeboat drill for the *James and Mary Walker* in the summer of 1910, with Walter Reekie's boatyard in the background. He also had a boatyard at St Monans. In 1949 Walter Reekie was drowned in St Monans harbour, and his Anstruther yard was sold the following year to Alexander Aitken. The site was cleared in the 1970s and turned into a car park. At the time of writing it is the subject of controversial proposals to build a shed to house the Fisheries Museum's Zulu vessel the *Research*.

The courtyard of the Scottish Fisheries Museum, photographed in 1937 when it was part of Alex Cunningham's ships' chandler business. The site's association with fishing can be traced back to 1318, when William de Candela, the feudal lord of the town, granted this and other lands to the Cistercian monks of Balmerino. The monks built booths for fishermen and allowed them to dry their nets here, in return for which they had to pay the abbey 100 salt herring for every barrel cured. In the early 15th century the order built a chapel here dedicated to St Ayle or Agilus. When this was demolished to make way for a cooperage around 1850, the lancet window on the left of the picture was saved and incorporated in the new building.

The abbey leased its Anstruther property to one Thomas Wood in 1535, with a condition that he was 'to receive the Abbot and Monks of Balmerino in kindly hospitality'. It is believed that the 'Abbot's Lodging', shown here in 1937, was built during his tenancy. Following Alex Cunningham's retirement in 1968, a locally organised charitable trust was formed with the aim of converting the buildings into a museum. Restoration was begun in the same year by W. Murray Jack, and the first part of the Scottish Fisheries Museum was opened in July 1969. From modest beginnings it has grown into one of the most successful independent museums in Scotland.

HARBOUR HEAD ANSTRUTHER

An atmospheric and unusual picture of the Harbourhead, dating from the first decade of this century. The well worn forestair of the Sun Tavern has been replaced, and the old crowstepped house next door is now incorporated in the Fisheries Museum, although minus its curious porthole window.

Charles Burrows' mid-1920s photograph of Walker's Close off Shore Street, with a glimpse of the harbour as its focal point. Anster abounds in antique and quirky pends and many of them, including this one, have been faithfully restored.

Free Church & Middle Pier Anster

Modernised sailing Fifies with wheelhouses added date this picture to the 1920s. The tall tenement on the right was demolished in 1926 during slum clearance operations in Hadfoot Wynd and East Green.

CHALMERS MEMORIAL CHURCH, ANSTRUTHER.

19474. J.V.

Thomas Chalmers was born in Anstruther in 1780, and at the age of just twelve began his studies at St Andrews University. He was ordained minister of Kilmany parish in 1803. In 1814 he was called to the Tron parish of Glasgow, and during the next two decades enjoyed a glittering and prestigious career. In the 1830s he became Convener of the Church Extension Comittee, a body dedicated to raising funds for the creation of new churches, and in the seven years he held the post enough cash was amassed for over 200 buildings. But Chalmers, like many other ministers of his day, was becoming increasingly unhappy at what he saw as state interference in the affairs of the Kirk. In 1843 he headed the 'Disruption', when 470 ministers left the Established Church and formed the Free Church of Scotland. Chalmers was the first moderator of the breakaway sect, and founded a church and school at Edinburgh's West Port. From 1845 until his death two years later he was Principal of the new Free Church College for the training of ministers. The Chalmers' Memorial Church was completed in 1891 to plans drawn up by David Henry of St Andrews, who also designed the Waid Academy. This massive pile dominated the Anstruther skyline for a century, its spire so prominent that it featured as a landmark on navigation charts of the Forth.

Chalmers Memorial Church, Anstruther.

The reunification of the Free and Established Churches in the 1920s left the Church of Scotland with a surplus of church buildings, a problem compounded by declining congregations over the ensuing decades. The Chalmers' Memorial was eventually closed for worship in 1978, and the 'B' listed building passed through a number of owners. Applications to tear it down were consistently refused, but on 10 May 1991, just a month after the 100th anniversary of its inaugural service, an unexplained blaze ripped through the church. Damage was so severe that demolition began just three days later. A housing development, appropriately called Chalmers' Brae, is currently being built on the site.

JAMES ST, CELLARDYKE.

Cellardyke was formerly known as Nether Kilrenny and Skinfasthaven, the first record of the name 'Syller Dyk' appearing in the Kirk Session register of Anstruther Wester in 1579. According to tradition the foundations of the place date back to an ancient time when fishermen living in Kilrenny built sheds on the foreshore here to store their gear, and as the village grew it became home to the majority of Anster's fishermen. This postcard dates from around 1910. The name James Street was adopted in 1873, in honour of James Fowler, a Cellardyke businessman. The buildings at the far end of the street housed Ingram's kippering works which were destroyed by fire in 1912, the site remaining vacant until the Harbourlea houses were erected in 1981.

The present Cellardyke Town Hall was donated by Stephen Williamson, and built in 1883 on the site of its seventeenth century predecessor. The architects were Hall and Henry. The pair of small, low houses on the left of the picture have recently been partly demolished.

John Street, seen here in 1904, was named by Provost John Martin in honour of himself in 1873. The cobbles were laid from the Town hall to Cellardyke harbour in 1868 to combat damage to the street caused by large numbers of carts transporting fish.

Cellardyke, photographed from the air in the early 1920s. On the left are the school of 1872 and Parish Church, built ten years later. House building began in Forth Street in 1868, and the terraces of Rodger Street and Fowler Street were added in 1872.

Cellardyke harbour can be traced back to 1543, with a pier possibly predating it by a hundred years. In 1665 the defences were 'totallie demolished' by storms, and remained unrepaired until after 1668. They were largely rebuilt between 1829 and 1831, with a new quay being added in 1853. But from the 1860s onwards the Cellardyke fishermen rapidly began to adopt larger Fifie and decked boats. Anstruther harbour was far better suited to these, and Cellardyke was almost abandoned. By the time this enchanting picture was taken around 1895, this once teeming harbour was home only to a few small yawls.

The Harbour, Cellardyke

The fluctuating roof lines of the harbourhead illustrate changing centuries and fortunes. The dormer windowed blocks date from the late nineteenth century and replaced low roofed, seventeenth to eighteenth century houses with forestairs, like the one on the page opposite. The houses on the far right were built on the site of a ruin between 1904 and 1907.

The ancient cottage and the adjacent ruin, which had been roofless for at least forty years, were demolished when Shore Wynd was widened in the 1930s. The block on the left stands on the site of the mansion house built here for Bishop Kennedy of St Andrews in 1452; 'a stately tenement, supported by a tier of massive arches' and protected by the pier, which was allegedly built for the purpose. During its demolition in the late nineteenth century, the discovery and destruction of what may have been fifteenth century frescoes was casually reported. The photograph dates from the mid 1920s.

Forth Street. Cellardyke.

Houses were being built in West Forth Street in 1901, and soil removed from the site was used to fill in the 'Caddies Burn', which had once marked the boundary between Anstruther and Cellardyke, where East Green meets James Street. This 1905 postcard is rare, perhaps because the buying public were not attracted by the two rather prominent boys with their digits firmly lodged in their nostrils!

BATHING POOL, CELLARDYKE.

A.759.

The natural rock formation, adapted into Cellardyke bathing pond, was once known as 'The Shaulds'. The pool was completed by Robert Terras in 1932, and formally opened as the 'Cardinal's Steps' the following year. The diving boards and changing huts were all removed some years ago, and it is now, officially at least, disused.

Yawls in Cellardyke Harbour c. 1925. These were the smallest class of boats, and were generally used for inshore "small line" fishing.

KILRENNY CHURCH, ANSTRUTHER

The old stone bridge at the bottom of Kirk Wynd has lost its parapets and is overgrown with weeds. Seen here in 1910, it once linked the village to the estate of Innergellie. Kilrenny is believed to be named after the saint to whom the church is dedicated, but his identity is far from conclusive. Most popular is the theory that he was St Irenaeus, an early Bishop of Lyons, but other sources suggest St Ethernan, who may or may not have been the same person as the ninth century St Adrian of the May Island.

KILRENNY NEAR ANSTRUTHER.

Most of these cottages have been given modern additions since this 1926 postcard was published. Before St Adrian's church in Anster was built in 1634, Kilrenny church served the whole of the parish, and would have been the focal point of the medieval community. Although few of its buildings appear to predate the seventeenth century, their occupants can be confident they stand on ancient feus.

Kilrenny's Rottenrow has adopted the more genteel name of Routine Row since this 1913 picture was posted. It has been suggested that the name is derived from 'route de roi', the King's way. Although the drainage has greatly improved, and the backs of these restored cottages are much extended, the outward appearance of this small street remains pleasingly unaltered.

The tower of 'St Irnie's', as Kilrenny Church was one known to its parishioners, dates from the fifteenth century, although the body of the church was entirely rebuilt between 1807 and 1808 to a design by Andrew Leslie. The porch was added to the front during remodelling by Gillespie and Scott in 1932. The school, immediately to the left of the church, was built in 1815, extended in 1841, and closed in the early 1930s. The adjacent schoolhouse was designed and built by William Lees in 1839-1840. Happily, Kilrenny has suffered very few architectural casualties, but both the forestaired houses in this Edwardian view have now gone.

Still looking very much the same today, this house and workshop at 11 Main Street, Kilrenny belonged to John Victor Heininen, cycle maker when this pre World War I picture was taken. His sign proclaims 'workmanship guaranteed, charges moderate, enamelling, plating & repairing'. As an adjunct to his trade he also advertises 'musical instruments can be had at the shortest notice'. Trade directories record Heininen in business here by 1907, and although listed in 1921 he does not appear in the subsequent 1928 edition.